THE FEEL BRAVE

GRATITUDE JOURNAL

1 DOSE/DAY

AVRIL MCDONALD

ILLUSTRATED BY TATIANA MININA

First published by Feel Brave Pty Ltd

www.feelbrave.com

© Avril McDonald 2023

The right of Avril McDonald to be identified as the author of this work has been asserted by her in accordance with the Copyright, Designs and Patents Act 1988

Illustrations by Tatiana Minina

First published 2023

Print ISBN: 978-0-6458846-3-0

This book belongs to:

....

Introduction

When we practise gratitude, it helps us to feel more positive emotions, improve our health, deal with adversity and build strong relationships.

This gratitude journal is designed to be shared between a child and a grown-up who loves them using the simple '1 Dose/Day' journaling activities.

Enjoy the daily connection and conversation openers with your little one and keep these precious written treasured memories forever.

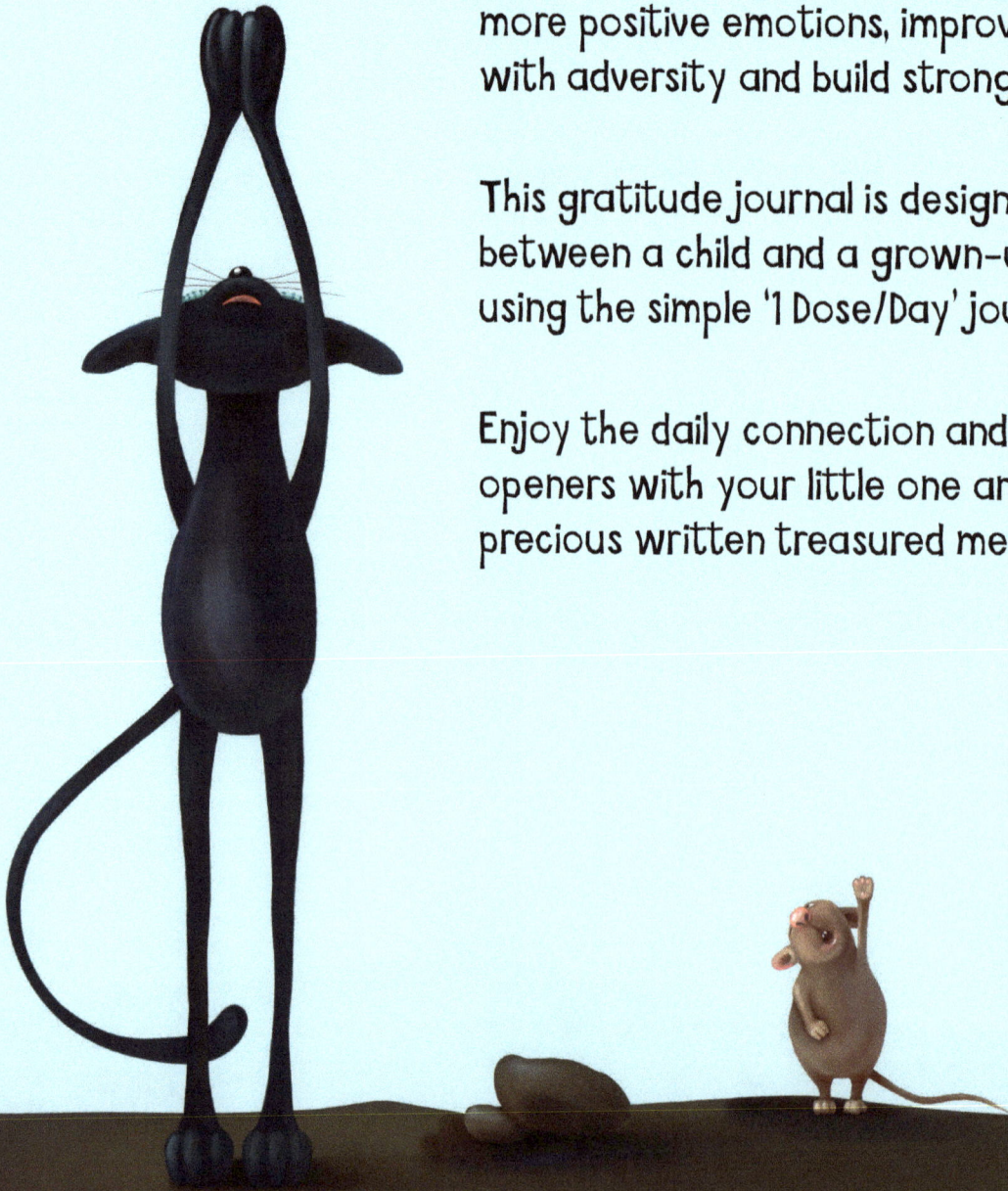

Before you begin

We can only ever start from where we are. Circle the face that shows how you feel for each question.

1. I like myself

2. I have lots of good friends

3. I know some good ways to calm myself down

Anything else?

. . . .

. . . .

. . . .

Daily Dose

Date: .. / .. / ..

AM: Today I am grateful for:

1. ....

2. ....

3. ....

Something I can do today that makes me feel good:

....

....

....

PM: Three things I did or saw today that were kind:

1. ....

2. ....

3. ....

Something to ponder on:

Where is the best place
you have ever been?

Daily Dose

Date: .. / .. / ..

AM: Today I am grateful for:

1. ....

2. ....

3. ....

Something I can do today that makes me feel good:

....

....

....

PM: Three things I did or saw today that were kind:

1. ....

2. ....

3. ....

Something to ponder on:

When have you felt really proud of yourself?

Daily Dose

Date: .. / .. / ..

AM: Today I am grateful for:

1. ....
2. ....
3. ....

Something I can do today that makes me feel good:

....

....

....

PM: Three things I did or saw today that were kind:

1. ....
2. ....
3. ....

Something to ponder on:

What makes you feel angry?
What is a good way to
manage an angry feeling?

Daily Dose

Date: .. / .. / ..

AM: Today I am grateful for:

1. . . . .
2. . . . .
3. . . . .

Something I can do today that makes me feel good:

. . . .

. . . .

. . . .

PM: Three things I did or saw today that were kind:

1. . . . .
2. . . . .
3. . . . .

Something to ponder on:

Have you had any interesting dreams lately? What were they about?

Daily Dose

Date: .. / .. / ..

AM: Today I am grateful for:

1. ....

2. ....

3. ....

Something I can do today that makes me feel good:

....

....

....

PM: Three things I did or saw today that were kind:

1. ....

2. ....

3. ....

Something to ponder on:

What is something about you that is different from other people?

Stars in the Night

A little poem to help calm a busy mind (this one is nice to do together just before you go to sleep).

Stars in the night, gather near
Fairies fly and meet us here.
As we close our eyes and count to 10
(shhh ... just whisper) 1, 2, 3, 4, 5, 6, 7, 8, 9, 10
Breathe in and out and in again
Wiggle your toes ... now make a smile.
Be very still and think a while ...
Who do you love and who loves you?
What's your FAVOURITE THING to do?
Where's the best place you've EVER been?
What's the most MAGICAL thing you've seen?
Now, stir all these things around in your cup
and like a hot chocolate ...
DRINK THEM UP!

Daily Dose

Date: .. / .. / ..

AM: Today I am grateful for:

1. ....

2. ....

3. ....

Something I can do today that makes me feel good:

....

....

....

PM: Three things I did or saw today that were kind:

1. ....

2. ....

3. ....

Something to ponder on:

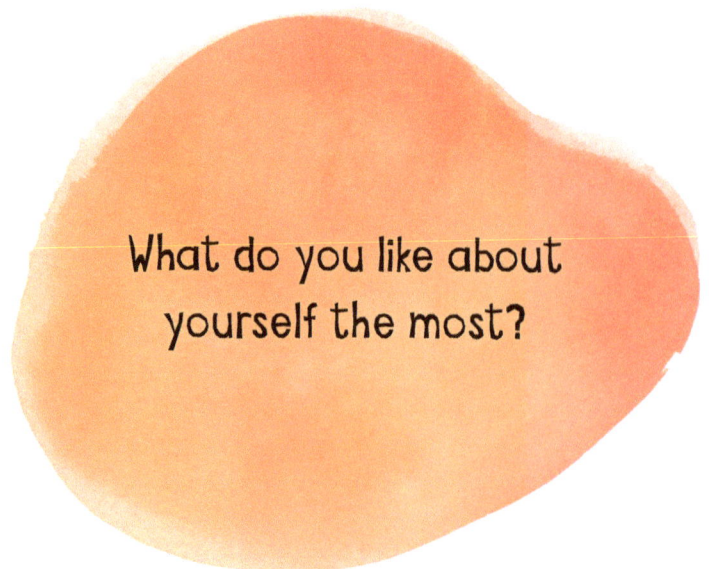

What do you like about yourself the most?

Daily Dose

Date: . . / . . / . .

AM: Today I am grateful for:

1. . . . .

2. . . . .

3. . . . .

Something I can do today that makes me feel good:

. . . .

. . . .

. . . .

PM: Three things I did or saw today that were kind:

1. . . . .

2. . . . .

3. . . . .

Something to ponder on:

What is your favourite animal and why? Is that animal like you in any way?

Daily Dose

Date: .. / .. / ..

AM: Today I am grateful for:

1. ....

2. ....

3. ....

Something I can do today that makes me feel good:

....

....

....

PM: Three things I did or saw today that were kind:

1. ....

2. ....

3. ....

Something to ponder on:

What is your favourite song? Would you like to sing a little bit of it together now?

Daily Dose

Date: .. / .. / ..

AM: Today I am grateful for:

1. ....

2. ....

3. ....

Something I can do today that makes me feel good:

....

....

....

PM: Three things I did or saw today that were kind:

1. ....

2. ....

3. ....

Something to ponder on:

What makes you feel the happiest? How can you bring a little happiness into your life every day?

Daily Dose

Date: .. / .. / ..

AM: Today I am grateful for:

1. ....
2. ....
3. ....

Something I can do today that makes me feel good:

....

....

....

PM: Three things I did or saw today that were kind:

1. ....
2. ....
3. ....

Something to ponder on:

Who is your favourite person and why?

I am a Tree

A little poem to help us stretch and calm down. Try doing it with the actions!

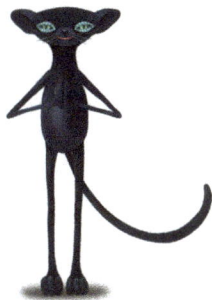

I am a tree. I stand tall in the ground.

As I reach for the sun, I will not make a sound.

I am the rain falling down from the sky

That wakes up the worm

who was sleeping nearby.

I am a mountain all covered in snow.

I am a seed

and I'm starting ...

to grow!

I am a tree. I stand tall in the ground.

As I reach for the sun.

I will not make a sound.

Daily Dose

Date: .. / .. / ..

AM: Today I am grateful for:

1. ....
2. ....
3. ....

Something I can do today that makes me feel good:

....

....

....

PM: Three things I did or saw today that were kind:

1. ....
2. ....
3. ....

Something to ponder on:

What would happen on your perfect day?

Daily Dose

Date: .. / .. / ..

AM: Today I am grateful for:

1. ....

2. ....

3. ....

Something I can do today that makes me feel good:

....

....

....

PM: Three things I did or saw today that were kind:

1. ....

2. ....

3. ....

Something to ponder on:

Do you know a funny joke? What is it? (It is always a good idea to have one funny joke up your sleeve!)

Daily Dose

Date: .. / .. / ..

AM: Today I am grateful for:

1. ....
2. ....
3. ....

Something I can do today that makes me feel good:

....

....

....

PM: Three things I did or saw today that were kind:

1. ....
2. ....
3. ....

Something to ponder on:

Describe one of your happiest memories.

Daily Dose

Date: .. / .. / ..

AM: Today I am grateful for:

1. ....

2. ....

3. ....

Something I can do today that makes me feel good:

....

....

....

PM: Three things I did or saw today that were kind:

1. ....

2. ....

3. ....

Something to ponder on:

If you could have one superpower, what would it be?

Daily Dose

Date: .. / .. / ..

AM: Today I am grateful for:

1. ....
2. ....
3. ....

Something I can do today that makes me feel good:

....

....

....

PM: Three things I did or saw today that were kind:

1. ....
2. ....
3. ....

Something to ponder on:

How can you help someone if you think they are feeling left out or sad?

Daily Dose

Date: .. / .. / ..

AM: Today I am grateful for:

1. ....

2. ....

3. ....

Something I can do today that makes me feel good:

....

....

....

PM: Three things I did or saw today that were kind:

1. ....

2. ....

3. ....

Something to ponder on:

When have you felt nervous? What are some good ways to cope with nervous feelings?

Daily Dose

Date: .. / .. / ..

AM: Today I am grateful for:

1. ....

2. ....

3. ....

Something I can do today that makes me feel good:

....

....

....

PM: Three things I did or saw today that were kind:

1. ....

2. ....

3. ....

Something to ponder on:

What is your favourite
day of the year?

Daily Dose

Date: .. / .. / ..

AM: Today I am grateful for:

1. ....

2. ....

3. ....

Something I can do today that makes me feel good:

....

....

....

PM: Three things I did or saw today that were kind:

1. ....

2. ....

3. ....

Something to ponder on:

Who is your best friend and why?

Daily Dose

Date: .. / .. / ..

AM: Today I am grateful for:

1. ....

2. ....

3. ....

Something I can do today that makes me feel good:

....

....

....

PM: Three things I did or saw today that were kind:

1. ....

2. ....

3. ....

Something to ponder on:

What is your favourite thing to do?

Daily Dose

Date: .. / .. / ..

AM: Today I am grateful for:

1. ....

2. ....

3. ....

Something I can do today that makes me feel good:

....

....

....

PM: Three things I did or saw today that were kind:

1. ....

2. ....

3. ....

Something to ponder on:

Who do you love and who loves you?

Random Acts of Kindness

A random act of kindness is when you do something kind for someone when they don't expect it.

Think of a random act of kindness that you can do for someone tomorrow.

Tomorrow night, report back on what you did and how it made you feel.

Daily Dose

Date: .. / .. / ..

AM: Today I am grateful for:

1. ....
2. ....
3. ....

Something I can do today that makes me feel good:

....

....

....

PM: Three things I did or saw today that were kind:

1. ....
2. ....
3. ....

Something to ponder on:

What is the most magical thing you have seen?

Daily Dose

Date: .. / .. / ..

AM: Today I am grateful for:

1. ....

2. ....

3. ....

Something I can do today that makes me feel good:

....

....

....

PM: Three things I did or saw today that were kind:

1. ....

2. ....

3. ....

Something to ponder on:

What do you want to be
when you grow up?

Daily Dose

Date: .. / .. / ..

AM: Today I am grateful for:

1. ....

2. ....

3. ....

Something I can do today that makes me feel good:

....

....

....

PM: Three things I did or saw today that were kind:

1. ....

2. ....

3. ....

Something to ponder on:

What is the best gift you have ever received?

Daily Dose

Date: .. / .. / ..

AM: Today I am grateful for:

1. ....

2. ....

3. ....

Something I can do today that makes me feel good:

....

....

....

PM: Three things I did or saw today that were kind:

1. ....

2. ....

3. ....

Something to ponder on:

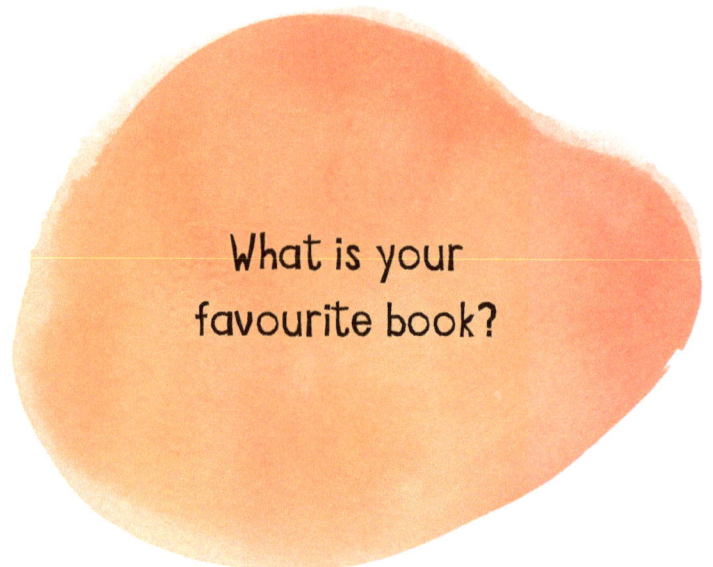

What is your favourite book?

Daily Dose

Date: .. / .. / ..

AM: Today I am grateful for:

1. ....

2. ....

3. ....

Something I can do today that makes me feel good:

....

....

....

PM: Three things I did or saw today that were kind:

1. ....

2. ....

3. ....

Something to ponder on:

If you could be any animal in the world, what animal would you be?

Daily Dose

Date: .. / .. / ..

AM: Today I am grateful for:

1. ....

2. ....

3. ....

Something I can do today that makes me feel good:

....

....

....

PM: Three things I did or saw today that were kind:

1. ....

2. ....

3. ....

Something to ponder on:

What do you think other people like about you the most?

Daily Dose

Date: .. / .. / ..

AM: Today I am grateful for:

1. ....

2. ....

3. ....

Something I can do today that makes me feel good:

....

....

....

PM: Three things I did or saw today that were kind:

1. ....

2. ....

3. ....

Something to ponder on:

Which person has said
the nicest thing about
you so far?

Daily Dose

Date: .. / .. / ..

AM: Today I am grateful for:

1. ....

2. ....

3. ....

Something I can do today that makes me feel good:

....

....

....

PM: Three things I did or saw today that were kind:

1. ....

2. ....

3. ....

Something to ponder on:

What is your favourite colour and why? What does this colour make you think of?

Daily Dose

Date: .. / .. / ..

AM: Today I am grateful for:

1. ....
2. ....
3. ....

Something I can do today that makes me feel good:

....

....

....

PM: Three things I did or saw today that were kind:

1. ....
2. ....
3. ....

Something to ponder on:

What (or who) really makes you laugh?

Daily Dose

Date: .. / .. / ..

AM: Today I am grateful for:

1. ....

2. ....

3. ....

Something I can do today that makes me feel good:

....

....

....

PM: Three things I did or saw today that were kind:

1. ....

2. ....

3. ....

Something to ponder on:

What is your favourite show? Why is it your favourite?

Have a little check in with yourself

See if your feelings are the same or different from when you started your gratitude journal. What do you notice?

1. I like myself

2. I have lots of good friends

3. I know some good ways to calm myself down

Anything else?

....

....

....

Daily Dose

Date: .. / .. / ..

AM: Today I am grateful for:

1. ....

2. ....

3. ....

Something I can do today that makes me feel good:

....

....

....

PM: Three things I did or saw today that were kind:

1. ....

2. ....

3. ....

Something to ponder on:

Who is the funniest person you know?

Daily Dose

Date: .. / .. / ..

AM: Today I am grateful for:

1. ....
2. ....
3. ....

Something I can do today that makes me feel good:

....

....

....

PM: Three things I did or saw today that were kind:

1. ....
2. ....
3. ....

Something to ponder on:

If you could have one wish come true, what would that wish be?

Daily Dose

Date: .. / .. / ..

AM: Today I am grateful for:

1. ....

2. ....

3. ....

Something I can do today that makes me feel good:

....

....

....

PM: Three things I did or saw today that were kind:

1. ....

2. ....

3. ....

Something to ponder on:

Can you remember what you dreamt about last night?

Daily Dose

Date: .. / .. / ..

AM: Today I am grateful for:

1. ....
2. ....
3. ....

Something I can do today that makes me feel good:

....

....

....

PM: Three things I did or saw today that were kind:

1. ....
2. ....
3. ....

Something to ponder on:

What is the biggest surprise
you have ever had?

Daily Dose

Date: .. / .. / ..

AM: Today I am grateful for:

1. ....

2. ....

3. ....

Something I can do today that makes me feel good:

....

....

....

PM: Three things I did or saw today that were kind:

1. ....

2. ....

3. ....

Something to ponder on:

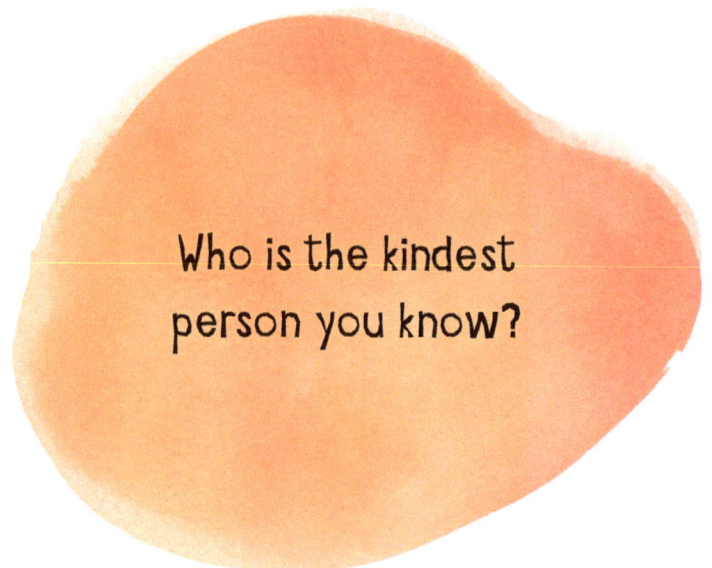

Who is the kindest person you know?

Mindful Time

Noticing things around us is a powerful way to help us refocus, be present and calm down. It is a great tool if we feel a bit anxious.

Take three nice big breaths in and let them out slowly making a hissing snake sound.

Now look around the room and notice and name five things out loud.

Daily Dose

Date: .. / .. / ..

AM: Today I am grateful for:

1. ....

2. ....

3. ....

Something I can do today that makes me feel good:

....

....

....

PM: Three things I did or saw today that were kind:

1. ....

2. ....

3. ....

Something to ponder on:

Do you like rainy days?
Why or why not?

Daily Dose

Date: .. / .. / ..

AM: Today I am grateful for:

1. ....

2. ....

3. ....

Something I can do today that makes me feel good:

....

....

....

PM: Three things I did or saw today that were kind:

1. ....

2. ....

3. ....

Something to ponder on:

Have you ever felt lonely?
What can we do if we
feel lonely?

Daily Dose

Date: .. / .. / ..

AM: Today I am grateful for:

1. ....

2. ....

3. ....

Something I can do today that makes me feel good:

....

....

....

PM: Three things I did or saw today that were kind:

1. ....

2. ....

3. ....

Something to ponder on:

Who is your favourite friend, and what makes them your favourite?

Daily Dose

Date: .. / .. / ..

AM: Today I am grateful for:

1. ....
2. ....
3. ....

Something I can do today that makes me feel good:

....

....

....

PM: Three things I did or saw today that were kind:

1. ....
2. ....
3. ....

Something to ponder on:

What is your favourite game to play?

Daily Dose

Date: .. / .. / ..

AM: Today I am grateful for:

1. ....

2. ....

3. ....

Something I can do today that makes me feel good:

....

....

....

PM: Three things I did or saw today that were kind:

1. ....

2. ....

3. ....

Something to ponder on:

Do you know any words
in another language?
What are they?

Daily Dose

Date: .. / .. / ..

AM: Today I am grateful for:

1. ....

2. ....

3. ....

Something I can do today that makes me feel good:

....

....

....

PM: Three things I did or saw today that were kind:

1. ....

2. ....

3. ....

Something to ponder on:

If you could make up your own language, how would you say: 'I love you'?

Daily Dose

Date: .. / .. / ..

AM: Today I am grateful for:

1. ....

2. ....

3. ....

Something I can do today that makes me feel good:

....

....

....

PM: Three things I did or saw today that were kind:

1. ....

2. ....

3. ....

Something to ponder on:

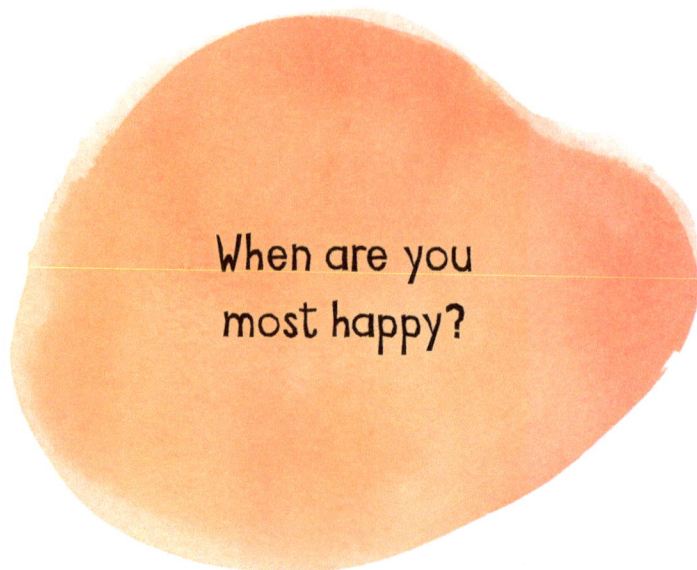

When are you
most happy?

Daily Dose

Date: .. / .. / ..

AM: Today I am grateful for:

1. ....

2. ....

3. ....

Something I can do today that makes me feel good:

....

....

....

PM: Three things I did or saw today that were kind:

1. ....

2. ....

3. ....

Something to ponder on:

If you could go on a holiday anywhere in the world, where would you like to go?

Daily Dose

Date: .. / .. / ..

AM: Today I am grateful for:

1. ....

2. ....

3. ....

Something I can do today that makes me feel good:

....

....

....

PM: Three things I did or saw today that were kind:

1. ....

2. ....

3. ....

Something to ponder on:

What famous person
or character would
you love to meet?

Daily Dose

Date: .. / .. / ..

AM: Today I am grateful for:

1. ....

2. ....

3. ....

Something I can do today that makes me feel good:

....

....

....

PM: Three things I did or saw today that were kind:

1. ....

2. ....

3. ....

Something to ponder on:

Can you cook a meal?
What meal would you like
to cook or learn to cook?

Candle Fingers

Little breathing techniques can help us if we feel anxious or nervous.

Imagine that your ten fingers are candles. Blow out each candle starting at your thumb and then each finger in turn.

Now, try blowing out your candle fingers again, but starting from your little finger and working your way back to your thumb.

How does this make you feel?

Daily Dose

Date: .. / .. / ..

AM: Today I am grateful for:

1. ....
2. ....
3. ....

Something I can do today that makes me feel good:

....

....

....

PM: Three things I did or saw today that were kind:

1. ....
2. ....
3. ....

Something to ponder on:

Which season is your favourite and why?

Daily Dose

Date: .. / .. / ..

AM: Today I am grateful for:

1. ....

2. ....

3. ....

Something I can do today that makes me feel good:

....

....

....

PM: Three things I did or saw today that were kind:

1. ....

2. ....

3. ....

Something to ponder on:

What is something you can do to help yourself if you feel worried?

Daily Dose

Date: .. / .. / ..

AM: Today I am grateful for:

1. ....
2. ....
3. ....

Something I can do today that makes me feel good:

....

....

....

PM: Three things I did or saw today that were kind:

1. ....
2. ....
3. ....

Something to ponder on:

What is your favourite toy?

Daily Dose

Date: .. / .. / ..

AM: Today I am grateful for:

1. ....

2. ....

3. ....

Something I can do today that makes me feel good:

....

....

....

PM: Three things I did or saw today that were kind:

1. ....

2. ....

3. ....

Something to ponder on:

What is the best name you can think of for a cat?

Daily Dose

Date: .. / .. / ..

AM: Today I am grateful for:

1. ....

2. ....

3. ....

Something I can do today that makes me feel good:

....

....

....

PM: Three things I did or saw today that were kind:

1. ....

2. ....

3. ....

Something to ponder on:

What always makes
your day better?

Daily Dose

Date: .. / .. / ..

AM: Today I am grateful for:

1. ....

2. ....

3. ....

Something I can do today that makes me feel good:

....

....

....

PM: Three things I did or saw today that were kind:

1. ....

2. ....

3. ....

Something to ponder on:

Do you have a pet?
If you do have a pet and
it could talk, what would
you like to ask it?

Daily Dose

Date: .. / .. / ..

AM: Today I am grateful for:

1. ....

2. ....

3. ....

Something I can do today that makes me feel good:

....

....

....

PM: Three things I did or saw today that were kind:

1. ....

2. ....

3. ....

Something to ponder on:

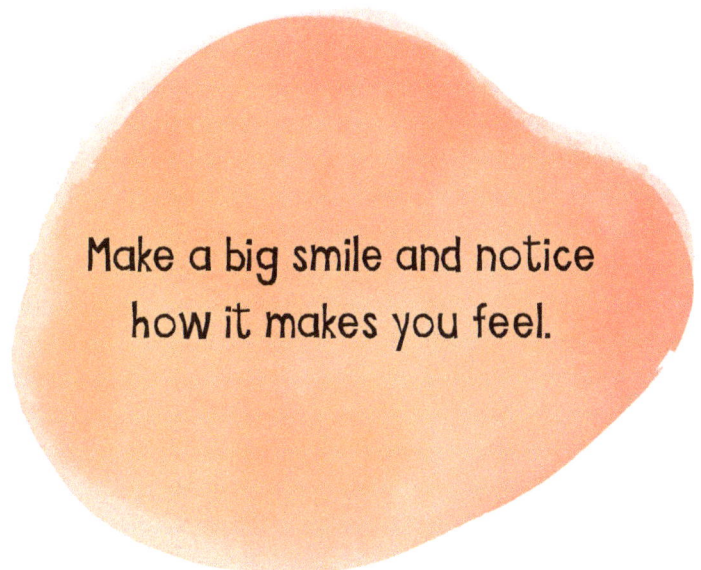

Make a big smile and notice
how it makes you feel.

Daily Dose

Date: .. / .. / ..

AM: Today I am grateful for:

1. ....

2. ....

3. ....

Something I can do today that makes me feel good:

....

....

....

PM: Three things I did or saw today that were kind:

1. ....

2. ....

3. ....

Something to ponder on:

What is your favourite day
of the week and why?

Daily Dose

Date: .. / .. / ..

AM: Today I am grateful for:

1. ....
2. ....
3. ....

Something I can do today that makes me feel good:

....

....

....

PM: Three things I did or saw today that were kind:

1. ....
2. ....
3. ....

Something to ponder on:

Who is your favourite superhero?

Daily Dose

Date: .. / .. / ..

AM: Today I am grateful for:

1. ....

2. ....

3. ....

Something I can do today that makes me feel good:

....

....

....

PM: Three things I did or saw today that were kind:

1. ....

2. ....

3. ....

Something to ponder on:

What is something new
that you learned today?

Daily Dose

Date: .. / .. / ..

AM: Today I am grateful for:

1. ....

2. ....

3. ....

Something I can do today that makes me feel good:

....

....

....

PM: Three things I did or saw today that were kind:

1. ....

2. ....

3. ....

Something to ponder on:

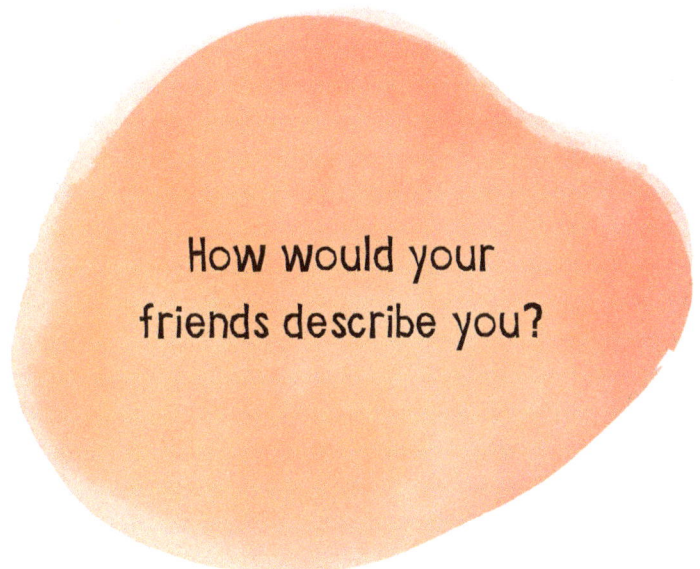

How would your friends describe you?

Daily Dose

Date: .. / .. / ..

AM: Today I am grateful for:

1. ....

2. ....

3. ....

Something I can do today that makes me feel good:

....

....

....

PM: Three things I did or saw today that were kind:

1. ....

2. ....

3. ....

Something to ponder on:

What is one of your favourite memories?

Daily Dose

Date: .. / .. / ..

AM: Today I am grateful for:

1. ....
2. ....
3. ....

Something I can do today that makes me feel good:

....
....
....

PM: Three things I did or saw today that were kind:

1. ....
2. ....
3. ....

Something to ponder on:

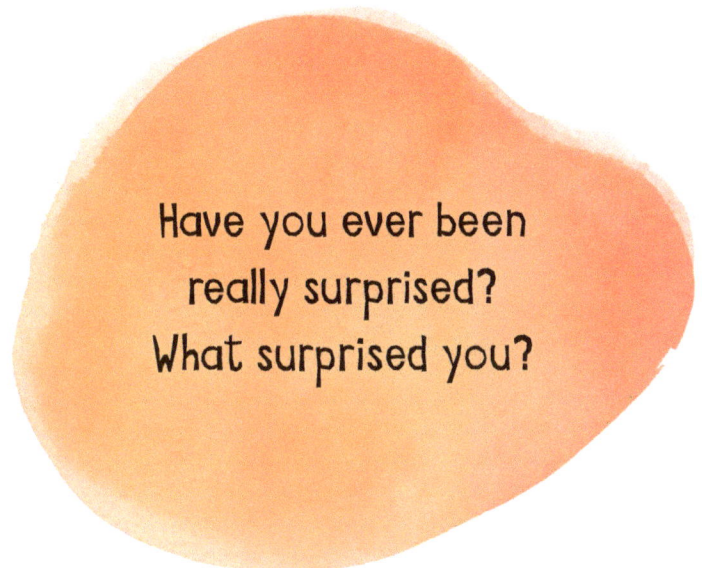

Have you ever been really surprised? What surprised you?

Daily Dose

Date: .. / .. / ..

AM: Today I am grateful for:

1. ....

2. ....

3. ....

Something I can do today that makes me feel good:

....

....

....

PM: Three things I did or saw today that were kind:

1. ....

2. ....

3. ....

Something to ponder on:

What is one of your favourite words?

Daily Dose

Date: .. / .. / ..

AM: Today I am grateful for:

1. ....

2. ....

3. ....

Something I can do today that makes me feel good:

....

....

....

PM: Three things I did or saw today that were kind:

1. ....

2. ....

3. ....

Something to ponder on:

What is your favourite instrument?

Have a little check in with yourself

See if your feelings are the same or different from when you checked in on yourself last time. What do you notice?

1. I like myself

2. I have lots of good friends

3. I know some good ways to calm myself down

Anything else?

....

....

....

Daily Dose

Date: .. / .. / ..

AM: Today I am grateful for:

1. ....

2. ....

3. ....

Something I can do today that makes me feel good:

....

....

....

PM: Three things I did or saw today that were kind:

1. ....

2. ....

3. ....

Something to ponder on:

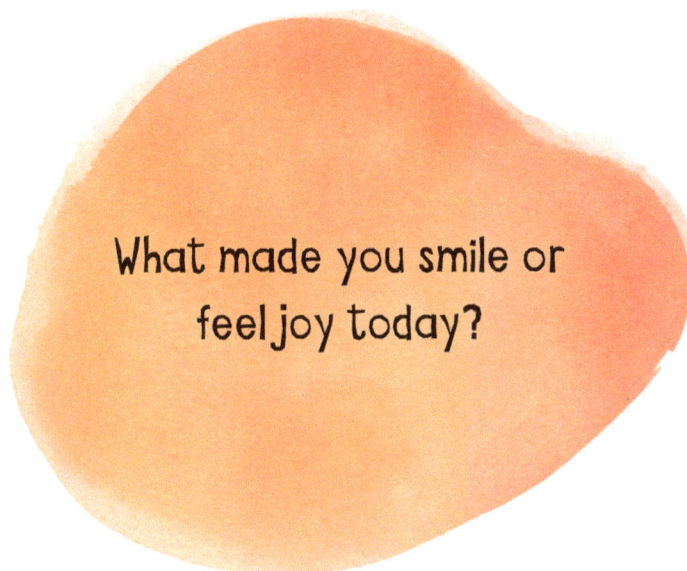

What made you smile or feel joy today?

Daily Dose

Date: .. / .. / ..

AM: Today I am grateful for:

1. ....
2. ....
3. ....

Something I can do today that makes me feel good:

....

....

....

PM: Three things I did or saw today that were kind:

1. ....
2. ....
3. ....

Something to ponder on:

What would you like to
be better at?

Daily Dose

Date: .. / .. / ..

AM: Today I am grateful for:

1. ....
2. ....
3. ....

Something I can do today that makes me feel good:

....

....

....

PM: Three things I did or saw today that were kind:

1. ....
2. ....
3. ....

Something to ponder on:

What would be your favourite imaginary place?

Daily Dose

Date: .. / .. / ..

AM: Today I am grateful for:

1. ....

2. ....

3. ....

Something I can do today that makes me feel good:

....

....

....

PM: Three things I did or saw today that were kind:

1. ....

2. ....

3. ....

Something to ponder on:

If you were the king or queen of the world, what would you change or do?

Daily Dose

Date: .. / .. / ..

AM: Today I am grateful for:

1. ....
2. ....
3. ....

Something I can do today that makes me feel good:

....

....

....

PM: Three things I did or saw today that were kind:

1. ....
2. ....
3. ....

Something to ponder on:

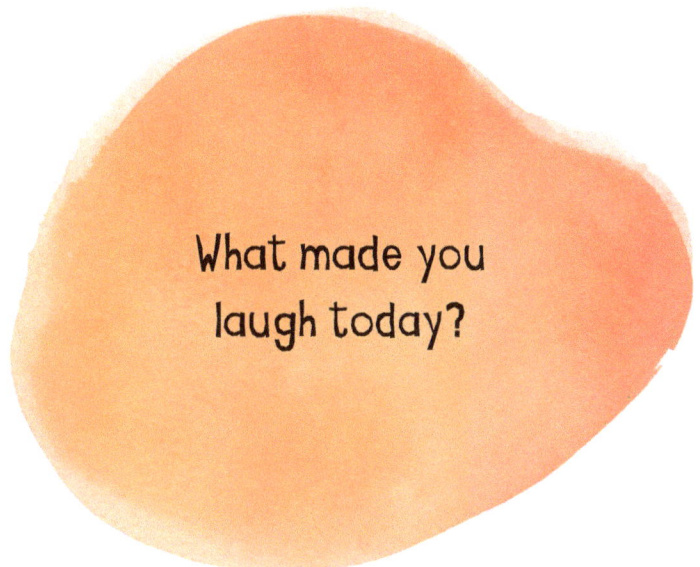

What made you
laugh today?

Daily Dose

Date: .. / .. / ..

AM: Today I am grateful for:

1. ....
2. ....
3. ....

Something I can do today that makes me feel good:

....

....

....

PM: Three things I did or saw today that were kind:

1. ....
2. ....
3. ....

Something to ponder on:

Name three things that
you love to eat.

Daily Dose

Date: .. / .. / ..

AM: Today I am grateful for:

1. ....

2. ....

3. ....

Something I can do today that makes me feel good:

....

....

....

PM: Three things I did or saw today that were kind:

1. ....

2. ....

3. ....

Something to ponder on:

What would your
ideal birthday party
celebration look like?

Daily Dose

Date: .. / .. / ..

AM: Today I am grateful for:

1. ....

2. ....

3. ....

Something I can do today that makes me feel good:

....

....

....

PM: Three things I did or saw today that were kind:

1. ....

2. ....

3. ....

Something to ponder on:

What is your favourite
type of cake?

Daily Dose

Date: .. / .. / ..

AM: Today I am grateful for:

1. ....
2. ....
3. ....

Something I can do today that makes me feel good:

....

....

....

PM: Three things I did or saw today that were kind:

1. ....
2. ....
3. ....

Something to ponder on:

How did you make
someone happy today?

Daily Dose

Date: .. / .. / ..

AM: Today I am grateful for:

1. ....

2. ....

3. ....

Something I can do today that makes me feel good:

....

....

....

PM: Three things I did or saw today that were kind:

1. ....

2. ....

3. ....

Something to ponder on:

Close your eyes and think of a very happy memory. Can you feel the happiness again?

Daily Dose

Date: .. / .. / ..

AM: Today I am grateful for:

1. ....
2. ....
3. ....

Something I can do today that makes me feel good:

....

....

....

PM: Three things I did or saw today that were kind:

1. ....
2. ....
3. ....

Something to ponder on:

Do you have a
favourite dance?
Can you do it now?

Daily Dose

Date: .. / .. / ..

AM: Today I am grateful for:

1. ....
2. ....
3. ....

Something I can do today that makes me feel good:

....

....

....

PM: Three things I did or saw today that were kind:

1. ....
2. ....
3. ....

Something to ponder on:

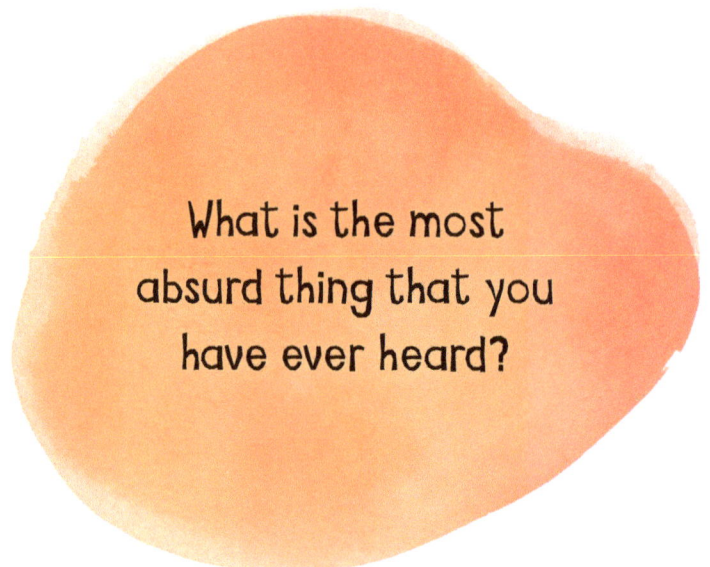

What is the most absurd thing that you have ever heard?

Daily Dose

Date: .. / .. / ..

AM: Today I am grateful for:

1. ....

2. ....

3. ....

Something I can do today that makes me feel good:

....

....

....

PM: Three things I did or saw today that were kind:

1. ....

2. ....

3. ....

Something to ponder on:

Which of your friends makes you laugh the hardest?

Daily Dose

Date: .. / .. / ..

AM: Today I am grateful for:

1. ....

2. ....

3. ....

Something I can do today that makes me feel good:

....

....

....

PM: Three things I did or saw today that were kind:

1. ....

2. ....

3. ....

Something to ponder on:

Who is your favourite
singer and why?

Daily Dose

Date: .. / .. / ..

AM: Today I am grateful for:

1. ....

2. ....

3. ....

Something I can do today that makes me feel good:

....

....

....

PM: Three things I did or saw today that were kind:

1. ....

2. ....

3. ....

Something to ponder on:

Can you pat your head and rub your tummy at the same time? Try it!

Daily Dose

Date: .. / .. / ..

AM: Today I am grateful for:

1. ....

2. ....

3. ....

Something I can do today that makes me feel good:

....

....

....

PM: Three things I did or saw today that were kind:

1. ....

2. ....

3. ....

Something to ponder on:

If you could have any animal in the world as your pet, what animal would you choose?

Daily Dose

Date: .. / .. / ..

AM: Today I am grateful for:

1. ....

2. ....

3. ....

Something I can do today that makes me feel good:

....

....

....

PM: Three things I did or saw today that were kind:

1. ....

2. ....

3. ....

Something to ponder on:

Can you name all the colours of the rainbow? When did you last see a rainbow?

Daily Dose

Date: .. / .. / ..

AM: Today I am grateful for:

1. ....

2. ....

3. ....

Something I can do today that makes me feel good:

....

....

....

PM: Three things I did or saw today that were kind:

1. ....

2. ....

3. ....

Something to ponder on:

Do you prefer breakfast, lunch or dinner?

Daily Dose

Date: .. / .. / ..

AM: Today I am grateful for:

1. ....

2. ....

3. ....

Something I can do today that makes me feel good:

....

....

....

PM: Three things I did or saw today that were kind:

1. ....

2. ....

3. ....

Something to ponder on:

What is your favourite way to calm down or relax?

Daily Dose

Date: .. / .. / ..

AM: Today I am grateful for:

1. ....

2. ....

3. ....

Something I can do today that makes me feel good:

....

....

....

PM: Three things I did or saw today that were kind:

1. ....

2. ....

3. ....

Something to ponder on:

What do you like the most about your bedroom?

Daily Dose

Date: .. / .. / ..

AM: Today I am grateful for:

1. ....

2. ....

3. ....

Something I can do today that makes me feel good:

....

....

....

PM: Three things I did or saw today that were kind:

1. ....

2. ....

3. ....

Something to ponder on:

Go through the alphabet and, for each letter, name someone you like or something you like to do. See if you can get to Z!

Daily Dose

Date: .. / .. / ..

AM: Today I am grateful for:

1. ....

2. ....

3. ....

Something I can do today that makes me feel good:

....

....

....

PM: Three things I did or saw today that were kind:

1. ....

2. ....

3. ....

Something to ponder on:

Can you make three superhero poses?

Daily Dose

Date: .. / .. / ..

AM: Today I am grateful for:

1. ....

2. ....

3. ....

Something I can do today that makes me feel good:

....

....

....

PM: Three things I did or saw today that were kind:

1. ....

2. ....

3. ....

Something to ponder on:

Name three people that you love and name three things about each person that you love about them.

Daily Dose

Date: .. / .. / ..

AM: Today I am grateful for:

1. ....

2. ....

3. ....

Something I can do today that makes me feel good:

....

....

....

PM: Three things I did or saw today that were kind:

1. ....

2. ....

3. ....

Something to ponder on:

Is there a special wish you'd like to make before you drift off to sleep?

Daily Dose

Date: .. / .. / ..

AM: Today I am grateful for:

1. ....

2. ....

3. ....

Something I can do today that makes me feel good:

....

....

....

PM: Three things I did or saw today that were kind:

1. ....

2. ....

3. ....

Something to ponder on:

What do you like better ...
sunrise or sunset?

Daily Dose

Date: .. / .. / ..

AM: Today I am grateful for:

1. ....

2. ....

3. ....

Something I can do today that makes me feel good:

....

....

....

PM: Three things I did or saw today that were kind:

1. ....

2. ....

3. ....

Something to ponder on:

What do you think is one of the most beautiful words in the world?

Daily Dose

Date: .. / .. / ..

AM: Today I am grateful for:

1. ....

2. ....

3. ....

Something I can do today that makes me feel good:

....

....

....

PM: Three things I did or saw today that were kind:

1. ....

2. ....

3. ....

Something to ponder on:

Do you have a favourite teacher? Why are they your favourite?

Daily Dose

Date: .. / .. / ..

AM: Today I am grateful for:

1. ....

2. ....

3. ....

Something I can do today that makes me feel good:

....

....

....

PM: Three things I did or saw today that were kind:

1. ....

2. ....

3. ....

Something to ponder on:

What is your favourite fairy tale, and why do you like it so much?

Daily Dose

Date: .. / .. / ..

AM: Today I am grateful for:

1. ....
2. ....
3. ....

Something I can do today that makes me feel good:

....

....

....

PM: Three things I did or saw today that were kind:

1. ....
2. ....
3. ....

Something to ponder on:

What animal do you think is the cutest in the world?

Daily Dose

Date: .. / .. / ..

AM: Today I am grateful for:

1. ....

2. ....

3. ....

Something I can do today that makes me feel good:

....

....

....

PM: Three things I did or saw today that were kind:

1. ....

2. ....

3. ....

Something to ponder on:

Where is your favourite place to be?

Have a little check in with yourself

See if your feelings are the same or different from when you started your gratitude journal. What do you notice?

1. I like myself

2. I have lots of good friends

3. I know some good ways to calm myself down

Anything else?

. . . .

. . . .

. . . .

Explore the other Feel Brave books:

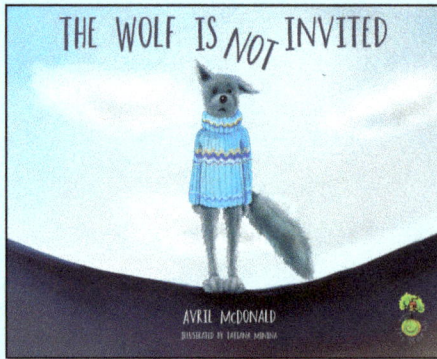

THE WOLF IS NOT INVITED
AVRIL McDONALD
ILLUSTRATED BY TATIANA MININA
ISBN: 978-178583017-4

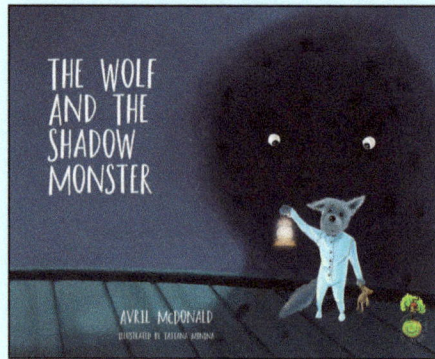

THE WOLF AND THE SHADOW MONSTER
AVRIL McDONALD
ILLUSTRATED BY TATIANA MININA
ISBN: 978-178583018-1

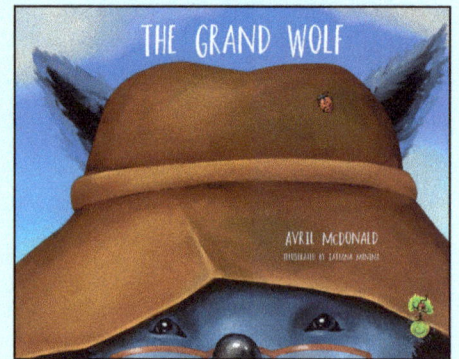

THE GRAND WOLF
AVRIL McDONALD
ILLUSTRATED BY TATIANA MININA
ISBN: 978-178583019-8

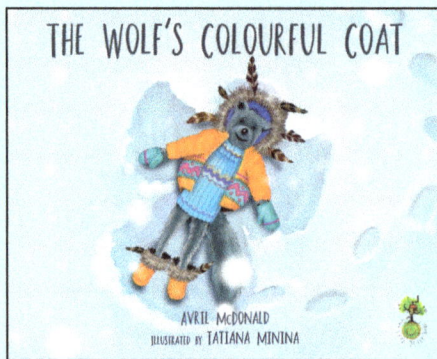

THE WOLF'S COLOURFUL COAT
AVRIL McDONALD
ILLUSTRATED BY TATIANA MININA
ISBN: 978-178583020-4

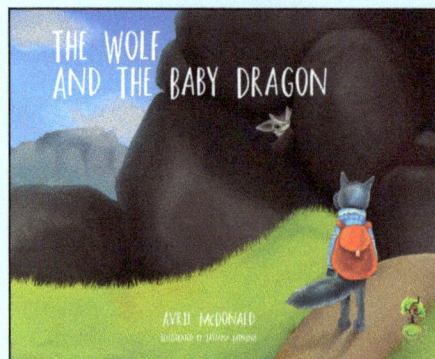

THE WOLF AND THE BABY DRAGON
AVRIL McDONALD
ILLUSTRATED BY TATIANA MININA
ISBN: 978-178583021-1

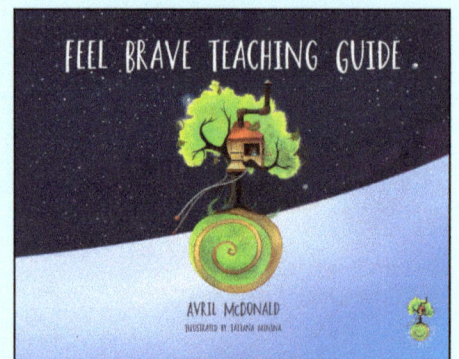

FEEL BRAVE TEACHING GUIDE
AVRIL McDONALD
ILLUSTRATED BY TATIANA MININA
ISBN: 978-178583016-7

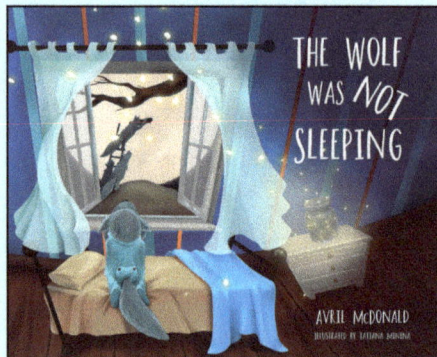

THE WOLF WAS NOT SLEEPING
AVRIL McDONALD
ILLUSTRATED BY TATIANA MININA
ISBN: 978-178583468-4

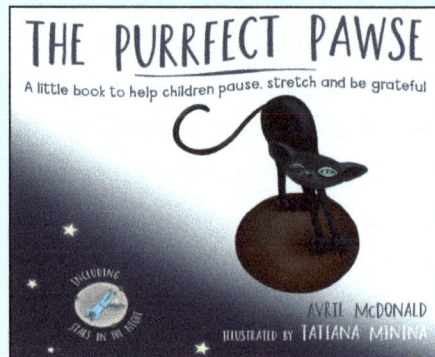

THE PURRFECT PAWSE
A little book to help children pause, stretch and be grateful
AVRIL McDONALD
ILLUSTRATED BY TATIANA MININA
ISBN: 978-178583333-5

THE PEOPLE'S BOOK PRIZE 2017 WINNER

era 2017 FINALIST

ForeWord Reviews 2016 FINALIST

Feel Brave Books

www.ingramcontent.com/pod-product-compliance
Lightning Source LLC
Chambersburg PA
CBHW040301100426
42811CB00011B/1328